Also available

Eat, Drink, and Be Merry
A Lamp on a Lampstand
Deceiving by Signs

Stand Still and Consider
A Commentary on Arguments in the Book of Job

By Lucas Doremus

First published 2020

Copyright © 2020 by Lucas Doremus

All rights reserved. No part of this publication may be reproduced, stored, or transmitted in any form or by any means, electronic, mechanical, photocopying, recording, scanning, or otherwise without written permission from the publisher. It is illegal to copy this book, post it to a website, or distribute it by any other means without permission.

All Scripture quotations taken from the New King James Version unless otherwise indicated.

Cover photo: "The Patient Job," Gerard Seghers, Public domain, via Wikimedia Commons

Cover design by Sarah Doremus

Second edition

Contents

Introduction	1
Chapter 1: Elihu's Discourse 32:1-37:24	4
Chapter 2: God's Discourse 38:1-41:34	21
Chapter 3: Examining Job the Person	27
Chapter 4: Job Argument 1 3:1-26	30
Chapter 5: Eliphaz Argument 1 4:1-5:27	32
Chapter 6: Job Argument 2 6:1-7:21	36
Chapter 7: Bildad Argument 1 8:1-22	39
Chapter 8: Job Argument 3 9:1-10:22	42
Chapter 9: Zophar Argument 1 11:1-20	46
Chapter 10: Job Argument 4 12:1-14:22	49
Chapter 11: Eliphaz Argument 2 15:1-35	54
Chapter 12: Job Argument 5 16:1-17:16	57
Chapter 13: Bildad Argument 2 18:1-21	60
Chapter 14: Job Argument 6 19:1-29	63

Chapter 15: Zophar Argument 2 20:1-29	65
Chapter 16: Job Argument 7 21:1-34	67
Chapter 17: Eliphaz Argument 3 22:1-30	72
Chapter 18: Job Argument 8 23:1-24:25	75
Chapter 19: Bildad Argument 3 25:1-6	83
Chapter 20: Job Argument 9 26:1-31:40	85
Chapter 21: Job's Responses to God 40:3-5, 42:1-6	92
Chapter 22: Epilogue 42:7-17	94
Chapter 23: Job Timing Indications	96
Arguments of Job in Summary Form	102

To Dick Chamberlain,
What sayeth the Scripture?

After the words of Job were ended in Job 31:40, The Word of God gives us this editorial comment: "So these three men ceased answering Job, because he was righteous in his own eyes" (Job 32:1).

Throughout Elihu's discourse to answer Job rightly, he gives Job only one command other than asking him to listen to his words multiple times. The command is this:

"Listen to this, O Job;
Stand still and consider the wondrous works of God."
37:14

Now if Job is the earliest book of the Bible written, and it probably is, and if Job had a worse predicament than any other human in history, and he probably did, then it is very interesting that God, communicating through Elihu, does not tell him to do anything but think about His Own works.

And now thousands of years later, whether our life is prospering or full of strife, we should heed this command to stop what we are doing and think about what God has done, what He is doing, and what He will do.

Introduction

Job can be a tricky book to understand, especially when starting at the beginning with Job's first discourse. Job and his three friends, Eliphaz, Bildad, and Zophar, all say true things but also say things that are untrue. Thankfully for us, the book gives us these editorial comments before Elihu begins his discourse:

> [Elihu's] wrath was aroused because [Job] justified himself rather than God. Also against [Job's] three friends [Elihu's] wrath was aroused, because they had found no answer, and yet had condemned Job.
> *Job 32:2-3* (emphasis added)

From this we know that all of Job's arguments in one way or another justify himself rather than God.

We also know that the arguments of Job's friends are trying to argue against Job's self-righteousness by pointing out what they assume is Job's hidden wickedness, condemning him without answering his arguments. Each man makes true propositions about God and the world, but their goal is not to justify or represent God truthfully. Instead it is to either justify self-righteousness (Job) or condemn a man for perceived sin (Job's friends). Armed with this understanding, we can properly discern what Job and his friends are saying.

Even though we have this framing, it can still be difficult to discern what Job and his friends have wrong in their discourses. Therefore, I have decided to begin with Elihu and his discourse because we know what he says about God, His actions and His character, are accurate in his conclusions. Elihu even summarizes different points Job makes in 33:8-11, 34:5-6, 34:9, 35:3, helping us understand what Job is saying.

It is also important to understand whether Job deserved all the trouble that was brought to him. God and Satan make an agreement for Satan to test Job to see whether he is righteous only because God is protecting him (1:9-11, 2:4-5). One could say that Job was not responsible for nor committed sin that led to his family, possessions, and health being taken away. Therefore, he did not deserve to be put through this trial.

The problem with this argument is that it forgets

Introduction

a very basic principle about the identity of man: we are sinners and deserve hell. Job was born a sinner and deserves nothing but punishment just like every human. It is only by the grace of God that we receive anything good, which Elihu will explain (33:23-24). So, while it is true that Job did not *directly* do any specific sin that caused the events of the book, it is also true that Job could not do anything to *not deserve* those events. We should never ever think that we deserve anything other than hell but simply rely on the grace and mercy of God and Jesus' sacrifice on the cross.

Furthermore, the events of chapters 1 and 2 apparently are inconsequential as far as proving Job wrong and justifying God because neither God nor Elihu makes a reference to God and Satan's agreement. God is justified no matter what happens and God's motive for any trial that we are put through ultimately glorifies Him (not that we often know His motive anyway). God is the hero of every story in the Bible, especially the story of Job.

I have greatly enjoyed studying the book of Job and have learned much from the wisdom it contains. I hope you will grow in grace and truth through this book. The contents of this commentary will be greatly amplified the more familiar you are with Job, so I suggest reading it multiple times before continuing. Have fun and see you when you finish!

Chapter 1

Elihu's Discourse

32:1-37:24

Elihu spends quite a bit of time telling Job and his friends to listen to him in chapter 32. He respects the fact that he is much younger than the other men, and therefore has waited to speak (32:6). In these verses, Elihu recognizes that the breath of the Almighty gives men understanding, and since the other men have lived longer, there is more time for them to have listened to God, and therefore gain more wisdom (32:7-9). However, age only gives the potential to have more wisdom, and unfortunately men do not always gain wisdom throughout their many years.

Elihu then addresses Job's friends specifically and recognizes their unconvincing words and their silence (32:10-16). Throughout their discourses Elihu has barely been able to contain himself from speaking (32:17-22), much like Jeremiah in Jeremiah 20:9. Elihu clearly understood the principle of speaking at the correct time, which was written later in Proverbs 25:11: "A word fitly spoken is like apples of gold in settings of silver."

Elihu's First Address

Elihu returns to speaking directly to Job in 33:1-7. He summarizes part of Job's argument this way:

> I am pure, without transgression;
> I am innocent, and there is no iniquity in me.
> Yet He finds occasions against me, He counts me as His enemy;
> He puts my feet in the stocks, He watches all my paths.
> *Job 33:9-11*

Job is basically saying, "I am blameless but God is punishing me."

Elihu answers him with an argument Job also made, that God is greater than man (9:1-13). However, Elihu does not conclude with one of Job's other arguments that man is deserving of an explanation (10:2, 24:1). He rightly states that God "does not give an accounting of any of His words" (33:13). Since God is greater than man, the Greater (God) does not have to answer the lesser (man) for any of His actions. In fact, the lesser is in no position to question the Greater, which is why Elihu says "why do you contend with Him?" (33:13). Furthermore, it seems that God does explain Himself in different ways, but man does not perceive or notice it (33:14).

One way God speaks to us is in dreams and visions. He opens our ears to instruct us in order to turn us from our wicked deeds. The purpose of God's instruction is to ultimately keep us from wickedness and death (33:15-18). When we reject this instruction, which causes sin in our life, and then claim that we have no sin before God, we are not righteous as Job was not righteous.

In fact, we receive pain from this behavior, which is detailed in verses 19-22. Job considered this God's punishment. When we encounter similar circumstances, whether God is directly chastening us or allowing the natural consequences of our sin to punish us, God is not obligated to answer our complaint.

"But He gives more grace" (James 4:6). I'm always amazed how God gives us answers to our questions even after explaining that He is not obligated to do so. God has sent a mediator or messenger to show man God's uprightness (33:23), although Job says he has no mediator (9:33). This is an act of grace, or favor, that man (the lesser) does not deserve from God (the Greater). In fact, the Hebrew word translated "gracious" means "to bend or stoop in kindness to an inferior." I believe this is a reference to Christ's redemptive death, especially since Elihu and

Elihu: 32:1-37:24

Job knew they would one day see the face of God (19:27, 33:26). To some extent, men understood God redeemed man from his sin and would one day be in His presence very early in history. Paul makes reference to the gospel being preached to Abraham (Galatians 3:8), giving further evidence of man's early knowledge of redemption and the method of receiving it being faith.

It is true that the Mediator mentioned above justifies us eternally and that justification gives us entrance into the sanctifying redemption that God offers. I think it is very safe to assume that Job is saved, since God is pointing out his righteousness to Satan at the beginning of the book (1:8, 2:3). Therefore, Elihu would not be telling Job how to get saved, but rather how to return to intimate fellowship with God.

When man submits to God in faith after sin has damaged his fellowship with God, He restores man with His own righteousness (33:26). When Elihu says that "he shall see His face with joy" in verse 26, I believe the joy goes both ways as the language is not clear. Man will certainly be joyful to see God's face, but I believe God has joy in our submission as well.

Once man is redeemed, the correct response is to admit his sin to other men. This is an important witness and can be very powerful in keeping other men from the pit (33:27-29). A public confession of sin may also be another way that God speaks to us (33:14). In verse 29, Elihu says that God works this redemption three times with a man, making this redemption we have been discussing about sanctification rather than justification. This seems to be a poetic way to say God will do this as often as man needs it. Elihu then reminds Job to listen, and the purpose of Elihu's words is to justify Job (33:31-33). This brings us to Elihu's next summary of Job's words, in which he addresses Job friends and their arguments.

Elihu's Second Address

We know that Elihu is addressing Job's friends because the pronouns in chapter 34 are plural, such as in verse 1, "you wise men" and in verse 10, "you men of understanding." He returns to speaking with Job in chapter 35 because the pronouns change back to second person as they were in chapter 33. Job's friends "had found no answer, and yet had condemned Job" (32:3). Therefore this section is telling us how Job's friends were wrong in their statements.

Elihu restates Job's previous argument, and then adds two arguments to it. He says:

> "For Job has said, 'I am righteous,
> But God has taken away my justice;
> Should I lie concerning my right?
> My wound is incurable, though I am without transgression...

> It profits a man nothing that he should delight in God.'"
> *Job 34:5-6, 9*

When Elihu says that Job has a "right," he is talking about Job stating that if he was allowed to plead his case to God he could be delivered from God's injustice (9:32-35, 13:3, 13:15-16, 23:3-7). Job's friends have repeated to Job many times that if man would obey God, He would prosper him, in which they condemn Job in the process because of his lack of prosperity. Job responded with explaining how the wicked prosper (21:1-34, 24:2-25), a concept repeated in the Bible many times especially in the Psalms. Instead of answering Job from God's perspective, which is what Elihu is about to do, they doubled down to condemn Job and telling him to fix his own life through his behavior.

Elihu's response to Job's friends' argument against Job is that God always just and righteous (34:10) for He repays man according to his work (34:11-12). Elihu explains in verse 13 why God has the right to repay man: "Who gave Him charge over the earth or who appointed Him over the whole world?" Since no one gave God authority, He can do what He pleases. Man does not have a right to question this authority, which Elihu and God will explain more as the book of Job progresses.

Job's friends correctly explained that God repays man for his deeds, but instead of placing the reason for that repayment with God's authority, they said it was because of man's works. If this was the case and God only repaid good for good works and evil for evil works, then God would be tied to a system like karma in Hinduism. A system such as this removes God's authority because God would be obligated to man and his actions rather than ruling over him. Man would still complain to God because the good for good acts would not be good enough and the evil too evil. God would then have to justify the fairness of the repayment to man, which Elihu already stated He does not have to do (33:13).

Before moving forward with Elihu's argument, it is worth noting an intricacy about how God always repays man accordingly. In the previous argument, Elihu made the point that God is gracious to man (33:24). This grace or favor allows God the freedom to repay good (rewards) and bad (punishment) to man. If this grace didn't exist, God would always repay man with evil because even our righteous deeds are not good enough to deserve a good repayment from a perfect God (Isaiah 64:6). But because God shows us grace and provided a Mediator (33:23), we can accept that ransom payment (1 John 2:2), and those that do are able to receive rewards, or good, for their righteous acts (1 Corinthians 3:14). Therefore, the Bible is completely accurate in saying that God repays man accordingly, both to those who have accepted His grace and those who have rejected it. Even though this doctrine is not laid out in detail in

Elihu: 32:1-37:24

the book of Job, the ideas align perfectly with what God revealed later in His written Word. The Bible is amazing in its consistency and how thankful we are that God shows us grace!

Returning to Elihu's response to Job's friends, he states in 34:14-15 that God could take back His Spirit and breath, which sustains man's life, and all people would die. This is the first reason Elihu gives to support God's authority over man: God is the Creator and therefore can do what He wants with His creation. Job's friends correctly state that God is in charge of nature (5:10, 22:16), but they do not make the connection that the Creator has charge over the created.

Elihu next explains that we as sinful man have no right to tell God that He is governing unjustly (33:17). Then he uses the example of servants questioning their superior, indicating that this is not the proper order of a master-servant relationship. Furthermore, Elihu adds that God shows no favoritism because every person is God's creation. Each will live and die according to God's fairness (33:20). How thankful we can be that God does not show partiality, no matter our status or the sin in our life (Romans 2:11).

With this background of God's authority over His created beings, Elihu explains that God knows everything that happens in every person's life (33:21-22). Because of this, man cannot tell God anything that He doesn't already know. When God judges man, it is because man turned from God (33:24-28).

11

To put all of this together, God chastens man because of his rejection of God's ways, which is perfectly just and fair, and man cannot plead against this judgement because God already knows all their works. In addition to this, verses 29 and 30 explain that no one can usurp God's quietness/judgement because then hypocrites, meaning those who challenge God's judgement, would rule unjustly.

More than this, if a man would appeal his case before God, He is not obligated to do what man asks (34:31-33). In fact, if God were to grant these requests opposite of His will and judgment, that would make Him unjust and a hypocrite, just like the hypocrites in verse 30.

Elihu concludes his speech to Job's friends by equating them with Job's unrighteous answers (34:34-37). Both Job and his friends are not justifying God but justifying or condemning man. Either way, God is not the focus of their reasoning but man. And with this conclusion, Elihu returns to speaking directly to Job in his third discourse.

Elihu's Third Address

Elihu begins addressing Job (notice the switch to the second person pronoun) by giving us yet another summary of his arguments:

> "Do you say, 'My righteousness is more than God's?'

Elihu: 32:1-37:24

> For you say, 'What advantage will it be to You?
> What profit shall I have, more than if I had
> sinned?'"
> *Job 35:2-3*

When Elihu summarizes Job's argument by saying, "My righteousness is more than God's," he is connecting what he just said to Job's friends about God always being just with Job's complaint that God is not just to him. Job never said this verbatim, but by claiming that he is blameless and that he could plead his case before God and be delivered, he is implying that he is more righteous than God (23:3-7). Whenever we think we know better than God, we are de facto saying we are more righteous and just than He. Elihu is also reminding Job of his previous two arguments, that God does not give an account to man and that God is always just and righteous.

The second summary of Job's arguments is directly addressing the pride of Job, essentially saying to God "What's in it for me?" or "Why should I bother serving you? You won't get anything out of it and my life would be the same whether I serve you or not." How easy it is to question God when our lives aren't going well or we encounter trouble.

After the events of Job 1 and 2, Job did correctly explain in 2:10 how we are to handle adversity: "Shall we indeed accept good from God, and shall we not accept adversity?" Solomon said it this way in Ecclesiastes 7:14: "In the day of prosperity be joyful.

Stand Still and Consider

But in the day of adversity consider: surely God has appointed the one as well as the other, so that man can find out nothing that will come after him." Job's problem was that he did not keep this principle of trusting God through the good *and bad*. He lost hope that his situation would get better (30:26) and fell into sin by complaining and boasting against God beginning in chapter 3. May we remember Job's former words through all the things we encounter in our lives.

After Elihu's recap of Job's words, he proceeds to answer him but not before he reminds Job that the heavens and clouds are higher than each of them (35:4-5). I believe this is a reminder of where God has His abode and foreshadowing how Elihu will use creation to prove God's superiority to man. Since God is so much higher than man, God is not affected by any of man's actions, good or bad. Elihu makes this clear in four parallel statements in 35:6-7 and then states in verse 8 that our actions, good or bad, only affect us.

Through the end of the chapter, Elihu lays out the normal way that man deals with this fact or avoids it. When bad things happen, we cry out to God for help because we know He could fix it with His arm or power, but our pride keeps us from submitting to Him (35:9-12). God does not listen to this empty talk because we are not asking God to fix it His way but our way (35:13). Elihu assures us that God is working justly even though we may not see it, and we must wait for His timing (35:14). Since we don't see God acting in the way we demand, we complain that God is not doing His job, or He is doing his job incorrectly. We may not do so in as many words as Job, but our intent is the same: we know better than God what should be happening (35:15-16). Putting this all together, Elihu's point is that God is higher than men and their actions and consequences do not affect God's perfect justice and timing.

Relying on God's perfect justice and timing always strikes me as such a simple way to deal with the "problem of evil." The "problem of evil" argument takes many forms but basically says, "Why would a righteous God allow evil in the world?" Instead of giving us some beautifully woven philosophical argument, God basically responds that "I am taking care of it with My justice and timing; wait for Me." The "problem" is really not a problem to God because He will always deal with evil in the proper way and at the proper time, whether in this life or the next. The real "problem" is that we are not satisfied with how and when He does it!

Elihu's Fourth Address

Elihu continues to address Job with perfect knowledge (36:3-4). As a side note, I believe the only way that Elihu would have known this was perfect knowledge was God told him this knowledge. With no prior written word, God must have communicated to Elihu these exact truths. Since God speaks directly to Job to communicate truth, I think God spoke directly to Elihu as well.

The last great argument that Elihu gives to justify God is that God is completely fair and understanding. In 36:5, Elihu tells Job that God is all powerful or mighty, but that He shows no favoritism, or despises no one. He is mighty in strength of understanding, which means He understands what the wicked and the righteous are going through. He treats everyone fairly, whether wicked or righteous (36:6).

In the previous address, Elihu explained that God does not listen to our complaining when we think we are more just than Him (35:9-13). In 36:6-7, Elihu brings eternity into Job's view of God's justice. Justice will come to the oppressed, for they are seated on thrones in God's view. This is one of the times in the Bible where the past tense verbs are used to explain the certainty of something rather than whether something is occurring according to our timeline. As another example, Romans 8:30 calls us glorified because our glorification as believers is certain, not because we are currently experiencing glorification. Furthermore, since God does not reside in time, He can speak of our future state, seated on thrones or glorification, as past tense because to Him it has already happened (Romans 4:17).

Notice what is said about the wicked – their life is not preserved. Ecclesiastes 3:16 and 5:8 makes it clear that the wicked do prosper in this world and our

Elihu: 32:1-37:24

own experience should confirm this fact. But if we consider eternity, the wicked will get their justice while the righteous will receive their grace and rewards (Ecclesiastes 3:17). When we see the perversion of justice and the wicked prosper, may we be reminded of eternity and how God will bring all things into judgement.

Elihu then returns to temporal life in 36:8, addressing how the righteous should view themselves when they do encounter affliction. Elihu says that God will remind the oppressed that they have sinned (36:9). I believe that the sin God reminds them about doesn't indicate that it is responsible for their oppression, in the same way Job did not have a sin that directly caused his oppression. How interesting that even when the righteous are oppressed, we are to search our lives for sin and turn from it. Notice in verse 10, that we don't have to find the solution; God instructs us in what it takes to turn from our defiance.

Job, and us by extension, are supposed to obey and serve God, or as the old hymn says, "Trust and Obey." If we do this, God can give us prosperity and pleasures. If we do not obey, we will continue to be oppressed and eventually perish by the sword.

It's important to note here that the guarantee of prosperity or continued oppression (36:11-12) is not to be taken out of context and applied to the current age of grace. Much of the New Testament is devoted to God being with us through suffering and examples of men's lives in almost constant suffering. However, there was still prosperity in their lives. In Paul's case, even though he was in prison and flogged many times (which were only some sufferings), what an honor he received to be used to write so many books of the Bible and see so many saved through his witness. So, while I do believe God will prosper us in our service to Him, the pleasures He gives us may be more spiritual rather than physical. That doesn't mean God will not prosper us Church Age believers with earthly blessings, but we must not apply what is said to Job to mean our obedience will guarantee us earthly prosperity and pleasures.

In 36:13-14, Elihu returns to talking about the wicked, or hypocrites, and the justice they will receive. He says they will die in their youth, which I believe is an allusion to those whose sin leads to an early death (James 1:5). The Hebrew word translated "perverted persons" indicates those who practice sexual activity related to religious rituals or other cultural norms. This sexual activity can cause an early death from sexually transmitted disease, making an early death a possibility. Elihu then reminds Job again that God delivers the poor in affliction and teaches them while they are being oppressed (36:15).

With this reminder, Elihu tells Job what would have happened if he had not begun acting like the wicked: deliverance from his distress (36:16-17). Neither Job's riches nor his authority would deliver him since Job insisted on the wicked path (36:18-19).

Elihu tells him to not seek the night in verse 20, which is connected to when the wicked carry out their acts. In 36:21, Elihu explains that instead of accepting his affliction and listening to the instruction of God (36:10), he chose iniquity.

In 36:22-23, Elihu states the same truths he has been explaining throughout his discourses, but in a very simple way: God is greater than man and He is not subservient to any teacher or judge. Throughout the previous five chapters, Elihu has beautifully spoken on God's behalf to justify Him instead of man. Now he turns to God's works for Job to consider.

Elihu's Fifth Address

Elihu tells Job to magnify the work of God which all men have seen (36:24-25). This is clearly a reference to creation, of which Elihu is going to emphasize the difference aspects of weather. But first in 36:26 Elihu tells of God's eternality and that Job cannot fully understand or know Him. Elihu is not saying Job cannot know anything about God, especially since he has just spent time explaining who He is, but it is true that Job cannot understand many things about Him because of His vastness and greatness.

Elihu then tells us about the rain, snow, and winds that God commands with His voice and breath (36:32-37:6, 37:10-12). In the same way that Job knows many things about God but cannot know Him completely, he cannot fully understand how the weather works (36:29, 37:15-18). Even in our modern age of technology we still do not wholly understand the cycles of weather. By the weather, God determines man's as well as animals' course throughout the year (37:7-8). He also judges mankind with it (36:31, 37:13).

With this description, Elihu tells Job to "stand still and consider the wonderous works of God" (37:14). Not only has Elihu answered Job's arguments but has given him something by which to look at and marvel at the majesty of God in contrast to his own works (37:15-16). He even gets a bit sarcastic when he starts lobbing questions at Job to reproduce the works that God has done (38:19-22). Elihu is making the point that since God is so much greater than us, we cannot say anything against Him because of our lack of knowledge and ability (37:23).

Not being capable of anything that God performs with the atmosphere, Job can only praise Him for His works. God is unsearchable, excellent in power, judgement, and abundantly just, and does not oppress us but judges rightly and shows no partiality. Therefore, we should fear and show Him profound respect (37:23-24). May we learn this great lesson, that when we are faced with adversity, we cease striving to justify ourselves, but stand still and consider God's wonderous character and works as Elihu has instructed.

Chapter 2

God's Discourse

38:1-41:34

God's discourse begins with power; He speaks out of a whirlwind, probably what we would recognize as a tornado. In keeping with what Elihu said about God not having to answer for Himself to man, God never gives an argument justifying Himself to Job. He simply states that Job is not speaking with wisdom and then tells him to prepare himself for an interrogation (38:1-3).

God's First Address

In chapter 38, God spends the first half of this address on the works of creation of the earth and universe. God uses questions to make His point to Job, all of them emphasizing God's power and wisdom over Job's inability and foolishness.

Stand Still and Consider

1. Verses 38:4-7 – The earth
   - How the earth was created, including its foundation and size
2. Verses 38:8-11 – The sea
   - How the sea was given its boundaries and evaporation cycle
3. Verses 38:12-15 – The earth's rotation
   - How the sun interacts with the rotation of the Earth and causes sunrises and sunsets
4. Verses 38:16-18 – Summary
   - Summarizes the sea and Earth points, also adding how Job does not comprehend death
5. Verses 38:19-21 – Light and darkness
   - How light and dark interact and their sources
6. Verses 38:22-30 – Weather
   - How different aspects of weather are produced, including snow, hail, rainbows, winds, storms, rain, dew, and frost
   - God times weather to coincide with times of trouble such as battles and war
   - God causes the rain to fall where there are no people, making His plan infinitely more intricate than what man would consider useful or efficient
7. Verses 39:31-33 – The Heavens (Outer Space)
   - How God has placed stars to form constellations and controls the movements of bodies in our Solar System

God : 38:1-41:34

8. Verses 38:34-38 – Weather
   • Restatement of God's control of the weather, with emphasis on controlling the clouds

Between Elihu and God's explanation of Who is controlling the weather, we are left to conclude that nothing on Earth or beyond Earth happens by chance. God is very well in control of all things, which the apostle Paul would state many years later in Colossians 1:17.

In 38:39, God now turns His attention to the animal kingdom, pointing out different aspects of different creatures. Below is a chart detailing each animal spoken of.

Verse(s)	Animal
38:39-41	Lion
39:1-4	Goats and deer
39:5-8	Donkey
39:9-12	Ox
39:13-25	Ostrich
39:19-25	Horse
39:26	Hawk
39:27-30	Eagle

God then concludes His first address asking Job to answer all of the questions He has just asked (40:1-2). I wonder if there was a space of time in between 39:30 and 40:1, since it says, "the LORD answered Job." If this is the case, God may have waited for Job to answer and he was silent, probably overwhelmed and speechless. Job responds after verse 2, which will be detailed later. God's might has been proved, but He continues to question Job in His second discourse.

God's Second Address

God begins His second address in parallel with His first, speaking from a whirlwind and telling Job to prepare himself (40:6-7). Launching His first questioning between verses 7 and 14, God essentially tells Job to "prove it." If Job is going to tell God He is doing things wrong, then he should command creation, give himself majesty, punish the wicked and save himself. Or said another way, "If I am doing it wrong, then do it right yourself."

Whenever we are in a position where we think we know better than God, it is best to remember that we do not have the power that God has. We can control very little in this life. Even those things we think we are in control of, God is above our control of those things (Ecclesiastes 3:14-15). Thankfully, as Elihu has made the point, God is all righteous and will never judge unjustly. Therefore, it is better to trust God and His judgement, knowing that He will eventually account for everything that has gone on in this life and that He is glorified by all of it (Ecclesiastes 3:17, Romans 11:36).

God next talks about two animals called Behemoth and Leviathan (40:15-41:34). Without going into great detail to keep within the scope of this book, I think Behemoth is a dinosaur, probably of the sauropod kind, and Leviathan is some kind of marine reptile which we may not have found bones of yet. Whatever these two animals are, they are different from the animals listed before in chapter 39. The difference is in the awe that they inspire to an observer. Job is supposed to consider these animals and have his breath taken away by the majesty and wisdom of God that went into creating them. Leviathan is even said to be "king over all the children of pride," possibly indicating that God used Leviathan to keep man from being prideful. This obviously worked, because Job replies in chapter 42 by abhorring himself and repenting of all he said (42:6). I hope that God recreates animals such as these in the new heavens and new earth so we can experience His majesty through them!

To conclude God's two addresses, notice that God does not develop any sort of argument to prove His greatness over Job as Elihu does. He simply directs Job to all that He has done and that is sufficient to make His point. I once had a colleague who stated, "when we look at creation, there isn't a label on DNA, stars, or anything else that says 'Made by God.'"

Stand Still and Consider

While it is true that fossils aren't dug up with labels, tags, or stamps like this, apparently God has put His mark on creation in a way that we should see it as being "Made by God" or else He wouldn't use creation to display His attributes so that we are without excuse (Romans 1:20-21). We should praise God in the same way David praised Him in Psalm 8!

> O LORD, our Lord, how excellent is Your name in all the earth,
> Who have set Your glory above the heavens!...
> When I consider Your heavens, the work of Your fingers,
> The moon and the stars, which You have ordained,
> What is man that You are mindful of him,
> And the son of man that You visit him,
> For You have made him a little lower than the angels,
> And You have crowned him with glory and honor.
> *Psalm 8:1, 3-5*

Chapter 3

Examining Job the Person

When examining Job, it is clear that Job is saved or God would not be talking about his righteousness (1:8, 2:3). Because of this, Job is not to be interpreted as proving he had spurious faith or losing his salvation during his arguments. Job is and always will be saved throughout the book, but I think his actions and arguments are born out of his complete hopelessness.

There are five different Hebrew words translated "hope" in Job and these words are used twenty-one times. Each time the words are used they are translated "hope" except for "yachal" which is also translated "trusted" and "waited."

Job says in 6:11, "What strength do I have that I should hope?" and in 7:6, "My days... are spent without hope." In 14:14 Job states he will "wait, till my change comes," that change being death. Lastly,

Stand Still and Consider

30:26 reads, "But when I looked for good, evil came to me, and when I waited for light, then came darkness." When we link these verses together, Job is without hope because his situation isn't changing. If we step back and think about this, this is an accurate description of what makes any person lose hope: when things are bad, nothing changes.

I believe all of Job's questioning of God stems from his lack of hope. When all his family and possessions were lost and he was struck with boils, Job could say "Shall we indeed accept good from God, and shall we not accept adversity?" because he had hope his life would improve. After some time passed, at least a week plus time for Job's story to spread and reach his friends (2:11-13), Job lost hope because nothing changed, and he didn't die.

As we go through the rest of the book, we should always remember Job's hopelessness is motivating him. We should also learn to be steadfast in trusting God and wait for His timing, never losing hope.

> And those who know Your name will put their trust in You; for You, LORD, have not forsaken those who seek You.
> *Psalm 9:10*

> Lead me in Your truth and teach me, for You are the God of my salvation; on You I wait all the day.
> *Psalm 25:5*

But I will hope continually, and will praise You yet more and more.
Psalm 71:14

Chapter 4

Job Argument 1

3:1-26

Job's main point throughout his first discourse is wishing he had died at birth (3:1-19). Who can blame him? Job is in a worse state than probably any other human has ever been in the world. He has been stripped of everything except his wife, who is still living but has forsaken him (2:9). Would any of us act any different than Job?

In verse 13, Job begins talking about what he thought he would experience after death. He makes the same points as Solomon does in Ecclesiastes, that the dead cease from the trouble that is on the Earth (Ecclesiastes 4:2-3, 6:3-6, 9:5-6). Job doesn't differentiate between Heaven and Hell, but groups everyone together in Sheol or the grave. Because of this, we are not to build any doctrine from this section of soul sleep, universalism, or any other doctrine that denies clarity about what happens after we die. He is simply relating the afterlife to temporal life, in which he is correct that once you die, all the trouble of this life ceases.

His concluding statements starting at verse 20 lament that he is still alive and wishes he could die now. Since his life is full of trouble and he sees no end or rest, it would be better for him to die than to live. As we said in the previous paragraph, Job is not considering any aspects of the afterlife that could have been revealed to him in terms of torment or paradise. He is just wishing to die so the temporal pain he is experiencing will end (3:20-26).

Eliphaz has seen Job's torture and has heard him, and now he tries to "comfort" him (badly I might add!).

Chapter 5

Eliphaz Argument 1
4:1-27

Eliphaz begins his first statement very well and comforting; it is a shame he kept going after verse 6! In verse 1, Eliphaz recognizes the state Job is in and says that after what Job has just said, how can one not respond? He then encourages Job by reminding him that He has instructed and strengthened many people in times of their distress (4:3-4). But now that Job is experiencing trouble, Eliphaz, in the form of a question, shows Job that the same integrity and trust in God he showed with others should be his confidence now (4:5-6). What great words to remember when we encounter trouble! If only Eliphaz had stopped there...

And then Eliphaz starts digging into Job. Verses 8-11 make the point that anyone who is suffering is suffering because of their own iniquity. This is the first mention of the very common thread throughout

Eliphaz: 4:1-27

Job's friends' arguments that for every good action blessing is received and for every bad action evil is received. This basically equates to the Hindu idea of karma. The basic argument of Eliphaz and the others is that Job is receiving this trouble because of his sin. If Job would correct his own iniquity, God would again bless him. Eliphaz picks up this same line of reasoning in all of chapter 5 as well.

Remember from Elihu's response to Job's friends that their proposition is basically correct that God always repays man accordingly. What they miss is that God repays man according to His justice and timing. While everything will be repaid, God is not bound to repay according to our timeline nor in a way which we think is fair. This means that God might choose to let an unrighteous man prosper on earth but in the afterlife judge him accordingly in Hell. In the opposite way, God may let a righteous man suffer, such as Paul or any of the disciples, and repay them with rewards in Heaven. Furthermore, God is not required to immediately repay good when we do something righteous, which would make Him subservient to our actions and not His will. May we always remember that God will repay everyone according to their work and trust God's timing above our own.

Eliphaz next talks about a vision he had in which a spirit spoke with him (4:12-21). Considering Elihu talks about God communicating truth while men sleep (33:15-18), we could take Eliphaz at his word that this really happened, especially since the spirit who spoke to him communicates truth. Alternatively, Job could be calling his bluff in 7:14 by saying Eliphaz is trying to scare him with this vision. We aren't given enough information to know one way or the other, but either way we can still address the content of this vision.

The spirit correctly speaks with the implied answer of "no" that no man can be more righteous than God his Creator (4:17). In verse 18, the spirit speaks of God not putting trust in His servants, the angels. This is accurate because of Satan's rebellion and the angels he took with him, thus God charging those angels with error. Eliphaz makes a good point that if angels who were with God in Heaven had a choice of serving God or not, man who was made from the dust must be even more fallible than they (Angels no longer have this choice because Jesus states in Matthew 25:41 that Hell has been prepared for Satan and his angels). Especially, as Eliphaz concludes, since man dies and angels do not (4:20-21).

Eliphaz then calls Job to turn from his iniquity throughout chapter 5 and God will bless him. Notice again the direction of the action, that Job must fix himself and then God will fix his situation. While the general principle of many parts of the Bible explain that righteous actions do indeed produce blessing, it is not a guarantee and should not be how we counsel those in turmoil. We should instead follow Elihu's counsel, to stand still and consider the works of God (37:14), which will put our focus on Him and cause us to wait for His salvation, however or whenever that may occur.

Job, however, doesn't like this answer, and I would agree with him! For the person in distress, it is not comforting to be told how much you are a sinner and that is why you are experiencing trouble. Job even makes this argument in his next discourse.

Chapter 6

Job Argument 2

6:1-7:21

After Eliphaz does a terrible job of comforting him, Job responds by explaining how his situation has drained him from all hope. The first 7 verses of chapter 6 are summed up by his first words, "Oh, that my grief were fully weighed and my calamity laid with it on the scales!" Job, in his eyes, is being punished by God and he finds no enjoyment in anything in life. Job then restates his wishing to die in verses 8-10. Job concludes this section by saying he has no strength to offer him hope and that he cannot even help himself (6:11-13).

Job next makes an excellent point by which we should abide: when someone is afflicted we should show them kindness, not wrath (6:14-23). As Job says in verses 22-23, "Did I ever say, 'Bring something to me?' or 'Offer a bribe for me from your wealth?' or, 'Deliver me from the enemy's hand?' or, 'Redeem me from the hand of oppressors?'" When someone is in a similar state as Job with no hope, condemning them for their actions will not be heard with wise ears (Proverbs 25:12). Job did not ask for correction and clearly had no strength to hear it in his complaining. Instead, our speech should be "like apples of gold in settings of silver" (Proverbs 25:11), telling them to "stand still and consider the wonderous works of God" (37:14) if we are given the chance.

Unfortunately, Job continues his self-righteous words in verses 24-30 by getting sarcastic with Eliphaz to "teach [him] and [he] will hold his tongue" (6:24). Job proclaims that "[his] righteousness still stands" and he is able to discern incorrect speech (6:29-30).

He next re-explains his predicament, how hard life is on Earth and how the dead receive rest from temporal turmoil (7:1-10), much like Solomon explains in Ecclesiastes (Ecclesiastes 4:2-3, 6:3-6). Therefore, Job says in verse 11, he will not stop complaining in his bitterness and anguish. He does not need a protector (7:12) and then he brings up Eliphaz's vision mentioned in the last chapter. Job must have interpreted this statement by Eliphaz as a scare tactic, trying to make Job strangle himself to death to improve his life by his own works (7:14-16). We should never place this burden on someone in anguish, that if they would only try harder to be righteous and stop sinning their life would be better. Even if their own sin has gotten them into their predicament, we should still seek their restoration, not their destruction (7:17-21, Proverbs 10:11, 11:4, 12:18).

Job then explains that this burden will eventually kill him (7:21). To Job, Eliphaz has exalted himself above all men as a watcher or guardian through his judgement and instruction. Even though Job is still being self-righteous himself, it is true that we do not have the authority exalt to ourselves above other men. That does not mean we cannot correct other men, but we are not to take God's place as judge (Matthew 7:1-6). We should wait on the Lord and let Him use us as He sees fit for correction and give counsel to our fellow man.

Bildad now gets his first turn to speak and responds to Job with what he thinks is right.

Chapter 7

Bildad Argument 1

8:1-22

Bildad begins much like Eliphaz by making a very correct statement but continues with incorrect conclusions. This is a very common theme of all four men, which brings truth to the proverb, "In the multitude of words sin is not lacking, but he who restrains his lips is wise" (Proverbs 10:19). It is correct, as Bildad says in verse 3, that God does not subvert judgement. However, his conclusion from this proposition is wrong, that if Job would only seek God, God would awake for him and prosper him (8:4-7). As far as Job's sons are concerned, they are sinners just like the rest of us and don't deserve anything less than being cast away like they were. But just like Job, they did not do anything to directly deserve this treatment, so Bildad is also wrong about them.

In verse 8, Bildad begins talking about the "former age." I think this is referring to the time before the global flood, but I will make a case for this reason in the chapter devoted to the timing of Job. But for our purpose in this argument, Bildad is simply telling Job to consider those who have gone before them and the wisdom that is contained in their lives (8:8-10).

He makes an analogy in verse 11 that papyrus and reeds cannot grow without the right conditions (8:10-11). When the conditions are not right, the plants die before the other plants. In the same way that these plants die prematurely, the hypocrite will die or be destroyed before he can flourish (8:13-18). But, Bildad says in verse 19, those who are righteous will outlive the hypocrite and be blessed with laughing and rejoicing (8:19-22).

The above scenario is how Bildad tries to answer Job's hopelessness. Bildad uses the words hope, confidence, and trust as a connection to Job's previous discourse (8:13-14). Bildad is calling Job a hypocrite because Job says his is righteous (6:29) but is experiencing the judgement of the wicked (8:13-15). If Job would stop forgetting God and place his hope in Him, God would again bless him.

To restate what has been said, it is true that the general consequences of righteous living produce blessing, but God is under no obligation to prosper us when we walk in His paths. Bildad also makes the same mistake that Eliphaz makes, saying that getting out of bad situations is all about us either ceasing to sin or doing more good things. Our hope in our Creator is what helps us get through trouble, not

Bildad: 8:1-22

necessarily avoid or end it.

Interestingly, Job actually agrees with Bildad in his next discourse, but not skipping a beat, uses it as an opportunity to uphold his own righteousness rather than God's.

Chapter 8

Job Argument 3

9:1-10:22

Job begins his next argument by agreeing with Bildad using the question "how can a man be righteous before God?" (9:2) with the implied answer of "he can't." Also true is that no one can contend with God (9:3). Job and his friends all agree on this point, but what they conclude with this information is different and incorrect. In a similar way, many believers can explain the first half of the Gospel correctly, that man disobeyed God and deserves justice. However, most Gospel presentations conclude by asking the listener to do something for God, instead of only believing that Jesus has paid their sin penalty and gives them eternal life upon their moment of belief.

Eliphaz and Bildad have been similar in their first arguments and Zophar will follow the same pattern. They have correctly explained God's righteousness above man's, but instead of instructing Job to "stand still and consider" as Elihu did (37:14), they have told him to stop sinning in order to fix his life. Job also correctly explains God's righteousness but justified himself instead of God (32:2). May we always be careful to hear not only the propositions of a teacher's lesson, but also his conclusion and weigh it against Scripture.

Until verse 16, Job correctly explains God's position compared to man. God's wisdom and might (9:4) is displayed throughout His creation (9:5-10) and therefore He is able to judge without man being able to reason with Him (9:11-16). But then in verse 17, we see that Job is not explaining God's majesty to glorify Him, but to explain why he is able to justify himself.

Job says in verse 17 "He... multiplies my wounds without cause" (emphasis added). Then in verse 18, "He... fills me with bitterness." Job's argument for God punishing without cause and filling him with bitterness is found in verse 19 and 32-33:

> "[W]ho will appoint my day in court?...
> For He is not a man, as I am, that I may answer Him and we may go to court together.
> Nor is there any mediator between us, who may lay his hand on us both. "
> *Job 9:19, 32-33*

Job's point in this discourse is that since God's wisdom and might are so far above man, He cannot understand how His judgement impacts the life of a man (9:21-32). If there was a mediator between God and man that understood both, Job could speak with him, and that mediator could translate Job's argument to God. Then God would understand Job's point of view, therefore justifying Job. But without the mediator, Job is too terrified to speak directly to God (9:34-35). Since this mediator doesn't exist from Job's point of view, whether Job does good or bad, it is all the same, that "[God] destroys the blameless and the wicked" (9:22).

How marvelous that we do have this Mediator in Jesus Christ, both in our salvation and sanctification. Jesus satisfied the wrath of God by dying on the cross, thus giving us access to the Father through faith (Hebrews 7:24-27). But Jesus also lived a perfect life, and thus can sympathize with our weaknesses (Hebrews 4:15). Even though this revelation of Jesus came much later in history, we know from Elihu that God had already given man some sort of message in which to show man God's grace and deliver him from temporal death (33:23-24).

Job has yet to grasp this or forgot it in his suffering. He continues in chapter 10 with what he would say to God if given the chance (10:2). In 10:1, I think Job gives us insight into why he is saying what he is saying – his hate and bitterness of his life justifies his complaining. How often we act the same way when we are suffering. When we feel wronged, we also feel justified in complaining and speaking in that bitterness. May we not make the same mistake Job makes but cease our words and consider the wonderous works of God (37:14).

Job explains through the rest of the chapter in various ways how God cannot understand man because He is not man (10:4-12) and how God is punishing Job no matter what he does (10:13-17). He concludes the chapter with another plea to have died in the womb and to be left alone until he dies (10:18-22). Even though Job is wrong in justifying himself, it is hard to blame him because of his situation. May we comfort those in distress with wise words instead of judgmental ones.

Zophar then speaks up, following the same pattern as Eliphaz and Bildad: "Job, this is all your fault and you'd better fix it by you own works!"

Chapter 9

Zophar Argument 1

11:1-20

Zophar begins his first argument by taking the moral high ground (11:2-3) by summing up Job's argument thus far in verse 4, then saying that God is not doing enough to punish Job for his iniquity (11:5-6). Zophar, like his friends, is not seeking the health or restoration of a man in distress (Proverbs 12:18).

Zohpar's basic argument is man cannot understand Who God is (11:7-9) and God can punish wicked men without hinderance (11:10-12). On the surface, Zophar is correct about this point. It is true that man cannot understand the deep things of God but only what He has revealed to us, a principle laid out in Deuteronomy 29:29. It is also true that we cannot hinder God and His actions (Ecclesiastes 3:14-15).

Zophar goes wrong by telling Job how to act because of these truths – to clean up his own life and

God will bless him (11:13-20). In Ecclesiastes 3:14-15, Solomon explains that God acts so that man will fear Him. This fear/reverence is similar to Elihu's conclusion that Job should "stand still and consider the wonderful works of God" (37:14). Instead of seeing how God is acting and then trying "fix" whatever we don't like about it, whether in our own life or the world, we should trust God that He is working things out (Romans 8:28). Notice that Romans 8:28 doesn't say all things *are* good, but that they all *work out for* good. Better to trust God and work with His plan than to question Him and work against it.

In 11:15-17, Zophar even tells Job that he would "forget his misery" and that Job's life "would be brighter than noonday" if he would change his wicked ways (11:13-14). On the contrary, if Job was completely responsible for both joy and suffering in his life, his existence would be miserable because he would keep himself from enjoying consistent happiness. If it were true that for all good actions good was received and vice-versa, even when Job experienced the fruit of his own good actions there would always be the threat of suffering if he wavered from righteousness. What a terrible existence to always be walking such a tight line of righteousness to make sure you avoid suffering. I have come across believers who think this way. If they are honest, they are miserable because they have no security in their faith but rather a constant fear of doing wrong things.

Zophar is teaching something similar, saying in 11:18 that Job "would be secure, because there is hope" and in verse 19 "no one would make you afraid." But even Job in his complaining recognizes that no man can be righteous before God (9:1). It is alluring to think that if we just try harder or sin less we can make all our troubles go away with the hope of a better day. However, the whole situation of Job, that Satan and God made a deal to test him, proves this idea wrong because Job's actions did not directly put him in his predicament. We should always try to do more righteous acts and sin less (Romans 6:1-2), but not to improve our life's station. We should or shouldn't do things to give glory to God and build our trust in Him more everyday (Romans 6:11-14).

Zophar concludes the first discourse of each of Job's friends. Each of them in their arguments calls on Job to clean up his own life and everything will be better. In their next round of rebuttals, they will shift their focus away from telling Job to change his behavior to telling him how awful life is for the wicked. Job is not going to respond any better to this reasoning, but first he will give a long discourse to refute this idea. Again, he will seek to justify himself rather than God.

Chapter 10

Job Argument 4
12:1-14:22

Job seems to be quite frustrated with his "comforters" at this point. I think he may even be shouting given how he responds in the first three verses of chapter 12, saying that wisdom will die with them and he is not inferior. He says he is mocked (12:4) and then says in verse 5, "A lamp is despised in the thought of one who is at ease." The word "lamp" can also mean misfortune, and I believe Job is poetically saying that it is easy for those in comfortable positions in life to judge those who are not in favorable positions. Job is quite right about this, and Jesus validates the same point much later in history by saying, "And why do you look at the speck in your brother's eye, but do not consider the plank in your own eye?" (Matthew 7:3).

In verse 4, Job repeats his position of being blameless and just. Then he says, "The tents of robbers prosper, and those who provoke God are secure – in what God provides by His hand" (12:6). This is Job's first hint at the classic "problem of evil" which he will expound upon in chapters 21 and 24, but Job does not continue with this thought. Instead he answers his three friends' arguments by agreeing with them that all creation knows God is all powerful (12:7-8). Job says, "Who among all these does not know that the hand of the LORD has done this, in Whose hand is the life of every living thing, and the breath of all mankind?" (12:9-10). Job spends the rest of chapter 12 talking about God's wisdom and strength that oversees and controls all mankind's affairs.

After a bit of sarcasm again (13:1-2), Job concludes his argument by continuing his previous point, that since there is no mediator, he "desire[s] to reason with God" (13:3). Job calls his friends forgers of lies (13:4), then tells them of the justice they will incur from their deceit (13:5-12). Job is right that they are speaking wrong things, but he is no better. If we are going to claim that someone is wrong about their statements, we should make sure we are correct in our own arguments. Job has made himself a murky spring and polluted well because he has faltered before his wicked friends (Proverbs 25:26).

Job says in verse 13 that he does not care what may happen to him because of his words, which is not a good thing to claim (Proverbs 14:16). Job explains why he is going through the trouble of justifying himself by saying, "Why do I take my flesh in my teeth, and put my life in my hands?" (13:14). He gives us the answer in verse 15 with his famous statement, "Though He slay me, yet will I trust Him." What great advice that we should all abide by! Job's problem was he continued, "Even so, I will defend my own ways before Him." No matter how God treats us, we should always trust Him. Period.

Job's mistake, and often ours, is that we keep going and think we have some sort of argument or position that we can lobby against God. If Job would have not included "even so" and accepted both good and evil from God (2:10), that would be righteousness. May we remember to trust in God no matter the circumstances and not think there is something more to say.

Job then begins to speak with God, challenging Him to point out where Job has erred (13:20-23). I have written in my Bible next to this verse, "Never do this!" We should never challenge God to point out our sin because we think we are too righteous to deserve poor treatment in life. If we ask this, and God starts pointing out our sin, we would only be able to respond like Job: "I abhor myself, and repent in dust and ashes" (42:6).

Job accuses God of hiding Himself from answering him and talks about punishing him for his youthful iniquities (13:24-27). Job next states that a man's life is short (13:28-14:2). The complaining resumes by Job saying that God is in control of man's

Stand Still and Consider

life and sets limits for what man is capable of, both in changing his judgement from God and his day of death (14:3-5). Finally, Job asks for rest from all his troubles (14:6).

What hopelessness there would be if God was unjust and lorded over His creation like an uncaring dictator. Thankfully this is not the case! Elihu has already told us that God is completely fair (36:5) and repays men justly for their work (34:11-12). Job's problem was that he didn't like God's timing and how He dealt with him. Whenever we are going through trouble, we should try to see God's restoration, whether it happens in this life or the next (42:10, 2 Timothy 4:8).

In 14:7, Job talks about his lack of hope because he does not see the light of future restoration. He contrasts a man's life to a tree (14:7-9), that if a tree is cut down, other trees will sprout in its place, keeping the forest alive. But man has one life and when he dies, he will not awake again (14:10-12). Job then wishes for death in anticipation of his judgment after death (14:13-17). Job concludes his discourse by blaming God for his lack of hope in life (14:18-22).

Whenever I read Job's concluding remarks, I can't help but feel sorry for Job. When a man has lost everything, the only thing he can cling to is God. Yet how difficult that can be when you know He is the source of trouble as well as blessing. I pray that if we ever find ourselves in a position of hopelessness, we patiently wait for the hope of the appearing of our

Lord Jesus Christ (Titus 2:13).

Chapter 11

Eliphaz Argument 2

15:1-35

After all Job's friends have tried to tell Job to stop sinning but he did not listen, they now take a different approach starting with Eliphaz. They describe the wicked man's life; I suppose trying to get Job to realize that his life is one and the same. Not only does this line of reasoning not seek the health of one in distress (16:5), but it is not effective against someone who is righteous in their own eyes (32:1, Proverbs 13:10).

Eliphaz spends the first 13 verses of his discourse essentially calling Job foolish. He then says in verse 14, "What is man, that he could be pure? And he who is born of a woman, that he could be righteous?" I believe the "saints" in verse 15 are actually angels, because of the parallel statement in the second half of the verse about "the heavens not being pure in His sight." It wouldn't make sense to compare man to

Eliphaz: 15:1-35

planets and stars, and given that certain angels rebelled against God, I think this is the best interpretation of this verse. In verse 16, Eliphaz repeats the same question as verse 14 using the comparison of fallen angels

The implied answer to both questions is no, which is correct. No man can be righteous before God on his own merit. What is strange about Eliphaz posing this question is that in his previous argument, as well as Bildad and Zophar's, he indicated that man could be righteous before God if he would stop sinning and be more righteous. That is the same pitfall of those who preach a Gospel in which they say there is nothing that a person can do to be saved, yet call on that person to repent of their sins, commit or surrender their life, or whatever way they describe a change in behavior in order to go to Heaven. It cannot be both; either man cannot do anything to be righteous or we have some contribution to make. When we preach the Gospel whether to believers or unbelievers, make sure we are clear that faith alone saves and there is nothing before or after our moment of faith that can contribute or is required for our salvation.

Eliphaz then spends the rest of his discourse describing a wicked man's life (15:17-35). However, it is a very general description, and fitting Job's situation into it is difficult. For example, Job did not act defiantly against God (15:25), nor was Job writhing in pain all his days (15:20). Job in his following statements quickly catches onto this, which feeds his self-righteous argument. Instead of learning more from Job about why he is in this predicament and then seeking his health and not destruction (16:5), Eliphaz generalizes the state of Job's life. In terms of counseling, this generalization does not help the one in distress and also causes a lack of trust in the counselor, which is exactly how Job acts (16:2). When we are put in a position to counsel someone, it is important to learn everything about the situation and then give wise counsel that is specific (Proverbs 20:5).

Job next answers Eliphaz's folly appropriately, but also takes another stab at God by justifying himself.

Chapter 12

Job Argument 5

16:1-17:16

Job begins this discourse by calling his friends "miserable comforters" (16:2), and then gives some of the best counseling advice the Bible has to offer. Job advises:

> I also could speak as you do, if your soul were in my soul's place.
> I could heap up words against you, and shake my head at you;
> But I would strengthen you with my mouth, and the comfort of my lips would relieve your grief.
> *16:4-5*

Whenever we are talking with someone who is hurting, we should never judge them with a "holier than thou" approach. Instead we should comfort and strengthen them by pointing them to Who God is from His Word (37:14).

Between verses 6 and 14 Job blames God for all his troubles, which in a manner of speaking is correct. Even though God gave Satan charge over Job's possessions and his flesh (1:12, 2:6), God also claimed responsibility for what Satan had done (2:3). God even says in that verse that there is no cause to destroy Job! Yet Job's view on why God has done this is uninformed, when he says that God hates him (16:9). If only Job remembered what he said earlier that we should "accept good from God" and "accept adversity" (2:10).

Job then gets very emotional in talking about his exhaustion from his troubles (16:15-16). Job is correct about himself in verse 17 that there has not been any violence in his hands, but his prayer/argument has not been pure. Instead, he has desired to reason with God to justify himself rather than God (13:3). He is not looking to God to search the depths of his heart to reveal his pride but is holding onto that pride because of his bitterness (7:11). It is hard to blame Job for doing this, but we should be learning what not to do from Job even if we have similar circumstances.

Job ends with a lengthy description of his lack of hope (16:18-17:16). He wishes for a mediator (16:21), he wishes for death (17:1), and again recounts what has happened to him (17:6-9), and even throws one more jab at his comfortless friends (17:10). Job is probably the most broken man the world has known, and his comforters truly have been miserable.

Job: 16:1-17:16

Bildad doesn't get the hint that Job is not buying what they are selling but continues where Eliphaz left off in describing and condemning the wicked.

Chapter 13

Bildad Argument 2

18:1-21

Bildad in his second argument is apparently trying to get Job to look at his situation, specifically his dwelling place, and realize that he has been wicked. But first, Bildad must also be feeling the heat of the argument and accuses Job of inferring they are stupid (18:2-4). After that, he tells Job that the wicked's light, referring to his life being lit or clear of trouble, goes out in their tent (18:5-6).

Bildad continues to describe the trouble the wicked encounters as he goes through his land. There are traps all over (18:7-10) that make his life difficult and his fear of these troubles greatly affects him (18:11-14). He even has to share his land with intruders (18:15), suggesting that the troubles do not allow him to protect his dwelling. After the wicked man dies, there is no memory of him and his offspring are not able to keep the land (18:16-21).

Bildad: 18:1-21

While it would be easy to dismiss this argument because we know it does not describe Job's situation, Bildad is actually correct in a general sense. When we cross reference the book of Proverbs and what it says about what happens to the wicked, we find Bildad's argument is in line with Solomon's statements. These two proverbs sum up Bildad's argument well:

The house of the wicked will be overthrown,
But the tent of the upright will flourish.
Proverbs 14:11

Thorns and snares are in the way of the perverse;
He who guards his soul will be far from them.
Proverbs 22:5

Other statements that compliment Bildad's discourse are Proverbs 13:9, 28:10, 28:18, 26:27, 12:7, 21:10.

In order to synthesize these scriptures, we have to conclude the wicked generally do encounter bad circumstances, but the righteous can also have circumstances that look like the wicked's. Ecclesiastes makes this point when it says, "In the place of judgement, wickedness was there; and in the place of righteousness, iniquity was there" (Ecclesiastes 3:16). Either way, Solomon concludes that we should rejoice in our own works because that is our heritage from God (Ecclesiastes 3:22, 5:18). Paul takes it a step further saying he would boast and take pleasure in his infirmities because the power of Christ would rest upon him (2 Corinthians 12:9-10). Instead of doing what Job did (justifying himself), how great a witness for Christ we can be if we look at our suffering as an opportunity to show God's strength. If we are counseling someone who is suffering, may we not do what Bildad did (passing judgement), but help comfort them and talk about the wonderful works of God when appropriate (37:14).

Job understands what Bildad is saying but does not see himself as wicked. He sees the suffering as something unjust that God has done and explains this to us in his next argument.

Chapter 14

Job Argument 6

19:1-29

Job begins argument six much the same way he began other arguments by telling his friends how rotten they are (19:1-5). Job ends his opening remarks by the transitional statement that God has wronged him (19:6).

Between verses 7 and 20, Job basically repeats what Bildad said about his situation, albeit with different details, but instead of attributing it to his own wickedness, attributes it to God's injustice. He also gets poetic and embellishes at times, for example when he mentions the children of his own body even though his children have died (19:17, 1:18-19). Job closes this part of his argument by again telling his friends that they should have pity on him instead of persecuting him (19:21-22).

Verses 23-24 are some of my favorite verses in Job because it's so prophetic! See the chapter on Job's location for a theory about how Job's words could have come to be inscribed in a book.

The next three verses are amazing in its revelation about what early man knew about the afterlife. Job knows that his Redeemer is alive, which shows his awareness of a living Redeemer. Also, Job knows that this Redeemer will stand on the Earth (19:25). Job knows that after he dies, he will see God in some kind of body (notice the words "skin" and "flesh" in 19:26). He also yearns for this encounter, probably even more so now because of his suffering (19:27).

Job's remarks are in line with the judgement Enoch preached before the flood (Jude 14-15). I believe this shows the amazing consistency of the Bible, that what Enoch said passed through Noah and onto Job's generation, eventually finding its way to the pages of Scripture in Job and much later in Jude.

These statements in 19:25-27 show us that Job never gave up his faith in God but went down a sinful road of self-justification. Job in this sense is much like David, Peter, or any other person from the Bible that fell into sin even though they never stopped believing in God. I find great comfort in these situations because when I follow similar patterns, I know my Redeemer lives and forgives!

Job concludes his statements by chastising his friends again, even pronouncing judgement on them (19:28-29). Zophar speaks next and takes a different angle on the wicked man in trying to persuade Job to see himself as his three friends see him.

Chapter 15

Zophar Argument 2

20:1-29

Zophar's argument in many ways parallel's Bildad's previous argument, but instead of talking about the wicked man's dwelling, Zophar emphasizes the wicked man's heritage or portion in life. He begins by declaring the reproach against him made by Job and that he must answer the rebuke (20:2-3)

Zophar recognizes that the wicked man does have joy, but it is short lived (20:4-5). He makes the same point as Bildad in verses 6 through 11 that the wicked will not last in their dwelling and his offspring will not be able to keep it. For the rest of his argument, Zophar talks about the prosperity that evil has brought the wicked man not lasting, and God will punish him for it (20:12-29).

Zophar is trying to make Job see that since his suffering is being prolonged, he is experiencing the

Stand Still and Consider

judgment of the wicked. Zophar apparently thought this was the right time to point this out after hearing Job admit he is experiencing a wicked man's judgment. If I was in Job's place, I wouldn't be persuaded by this reasoning either because it doesn't address Job's point that God has done this to him unjustly.

However, Zophar is correct in a general sense just like Bildad; he accurately describes the path the wicked generally encounter. Another two proverbs summarize Job's friends' statements about the wicked:

> The labor of the righteous leads to life,
> the wages of the wicked to sin.
> *Proverbs 10:16*

> The violence of the wicked will destroy them because they refuse to do justice.
> *Proverbs 21:7*

Proverbs 10:2, 11:3, 11:18, 12:11, 13:25, 15:6, and 28:19 also are good references. The same lesson we learned from Bildad's previous argument, that we should comfort those in distress instead of passing judgment, can be applied here.

In Job's next argument, he takes the offensive and explains what we would call in modern terms "the problem of evil."

Chapter 16

Job Argument 7

21:1-34

After hearing each of his friends describe the wicked man's life in their own terms, Job really lets them have it by describing how he sees the wicked. After beginning his discourse in a similar way to his previous few arguments by disdaining his friends (21:1-5), he asks them three questions that we hear commonly repeated today. He even is scared when thinking about his propositions (21:6), which is a natural reaction to the problem of evil if one is without hope in this life.

Even though the questions Job asks are common in terms of why evil exists if God is a loving Creator, Job is not asking them from an unbeliever's standpoint. He recognizes the wicked will get the justice they have coming to them (21:19-20, 30-33). Remember also in Job 19:25-27 that Job knows he will see his Redeemer after his death. These two presuppositions make Job's argument more of a "believer's terrestrial problem of evil" rather than the typical problem of evil argument that is used to attack God. How much we as believers can learn from Job when we struggle with the same thing!

Job's first question is the basic problem of evil: Why do good things happen to bad people? Or as Job puts it, "Why do the wicked live and become old, yes, become mighty in power?" (21:7). Between verses 8 and 13 Job lays out how the wicked prosper in this life. He then explains the wicked's relationship to God, which Romans 1 will echo many years later. The wicked recognize there is a God, but they reject Him and want nothing to do with Him or His instruction. Since they are already prospering, they see no value in knowledge God offers (21:14-15). Little do they know that it is God who has given them their prosperity and not their own doing (21:16). Job then claims that "the counsel of the wicked is far from [him]" in the second half on verse 16, which is him saying that he did not derive this reasoning from the wicked.

Job asks one central question with parallel questions in verse 17, "How often is the lamp of the wicked put out? How often does their destruction come upon them, the sorrows God distributes in His anger?" After studying this section (21:17-21), I believe the KJV does the best job translating the passage. When read in the KJV, Job is answering his own question that the lamp of the wicked is put out only at the end of their life (Proverbs 24:20 comes to the same conclusion). When ruin comes upon the wicked, he knows that God is the one punishing him and his destruction will impact their children (21:18-21).

Job's final question, which is really a complaint masked as a question, is in verse 22: "Can anyone teach God knowledge since He judges them on high?" Job is complaining that since God is untouchable by man, no one can correct Him about how He deals out justice to both the righteous and the wicked. Death happens to both the good and evil man; the evil man having a full life and the good man having a bitter one (21:23-26). Solomon saw the same thing and recorded it many centuries later (Ecclesiastes 9:2).

Job concludes his statements by chastising his friends, calling them schemers and effectively calling them stupid because they do not see what is obvious to those on a road (21:27-29). Their words offer no comfort to Job (21:24), and at this point I doubt Job is expecting any.

Job's friends will not offer any answers to Job's questions in their following statements. Instead, Eliphaz will resort to personal attacks. Whenever we see a response that evades direct questions and instead destroys the person, we should know that we are dealing with foolishness (Proverbs 15:28).

However, Elihu answers each of these questions:

1. Why do the wicked live and become old, yes, become mighty in power?
   - Since God is above man, He will do things justly and man may not understand it (33:12-14). Furthermore, man will complain because he does not ask for things to be done correctly but asks God to fix things out of his own pride (35:9-16).
2. How often is the lamp of the wicked put out?
   - God is fair to both the wicked and righteous, but man does not understand God's timing. God judges with eternity in view, where the righteous will be blessed and the wicked will be punished, both according to their works (36:5-15).
3. Can anyone teach God knowledge since He judges those on high?
   - No, because God is the one who gives man wisdom and man has no wisdom to offer back to God. In fact, God delivers man when he strays from His commandments so that he will not die (33:15-30).

We don't know if Job changed his mind after hearing Elihu answer his questions. Depending on the suffering that a person is experiencing, they may not be thinking clearly to listen to reason that satisfies their lack of hope. However, we shouldn't judge them for an unwillingness to listen. Our main goal when talking with someone who is suffering is to comfort them, as Job has pointed out many times. We should know the answers to questions about why suffering exists and use them if given the proper opportunity, but restoring a person with godly hope is more important than giving philosophically correct answers. Let us not be miserable comforters (16:2) but instead friends that stick closer than a brother (Proverbs 28:24).

Chapter 17

Eliphaz Argument 3

22:1-30

Because Eliphaz and his friends are convinced that Job is suffering because of his secret wickedness, he does not have an answer to Job's questions, nor does he even attempt to respond to them. Instead, he personally attacks Job and again tells him to clean up his life.

The introduction to Eliphaz's argument is actually true, that God gains nothing by our righteousness (22:2-3), but he is saying this to point out Job's perceived wickedness without answering Job's argument, thus condemning him incorrectly (32:3). Elihu will make the same argument in 35:1-8, but his point is to show that man's actions only effect man, and when a man sees injustice, he should cry out to God for help and wisdom instead of thinking we know how to judge better than God (35:9-16).

Eliphaz next launches into personal attacks on

Eliphaz: 22:1-30

Job, calling out many iniquities Job has allegedly performed (22:4-11). Considering what God said about Job in 1:8 and 2:3, I doubt these are accurate accusations. Remember that Job did not think he was perfect (13:26), but the sins Eliphaz is accusing him of are the same in nature as his previous discourses but go beyond them in severity.

In 22:12-14, Eliphaz accurately represents Job's argument that because God is so high above man, He cannot understand him, which Job concludes that He judges incorrectly (9:32-25). Eliphaz then likens Job to the wicked who were killed by a flood in verses 15-18 (the global flood of Noah's day in my opinion). He even uses the same expression as Job did in 21:16 to give himself credibility, claiming that "the counsel of the wicked is far from me" (22:18). Furthermore, Eliphaz says, the righteous rejoice at the cutting down of the wicked (22:19-20). As a side note, we as believers should not be glad when the wicked are punished but instead should understand it as God's repaying of the wicked and alternatively appreciate the mercy He has given us (Proverbs 24:17-18, Romans 12:19-20, Ephesians 2:4-5).

Eliphaz concludes his discourse with a call for Job to change his behavior and God will bless him (22:21-30). This is the same advice all three friends had given Job in each of their first three statements. It wasn't effective in changing Job's mind the first three times, and it doesn't work this time. Job, I think, is so fed up with this rhetoric that he doesn't even acknowledge

Stand Still and Consider

Eliphaz's statements in his next discourse. In fact, Job is bolder in proclaiming his self-righteousness and continues his questioning of why bad things happen to good people.

Chapter 18

Job Argument 8
23:1-24:25

Job doesn't respond to anything Eliphaz said but starts with more self-loathing over his situation (23:2). He then begins his next argument and has extraordinary pride throughout chapter 23. Job continues his questioning of why he doesn't get to know what God does and why He does it.

Job believes that if he were able to know where to find God and argue with Him, he would be vindicated in his self-righteousness (23:2-7). Job recognizes that he cannot fight God (23:6), but his reasoning would "somehow" teach God that He is in the wrong (23:7). Job's pride goes so far as to even assert that he knows what God thinks (23:5). Since no person can know the mind of God (1 Corinthians 2:11), it is extremely prideful to think that we know how to do God's job better than He does. Since God is the only source of true wisdom (Proverbs 1:7,

Ecclesiastes 2:26, 1 Corinthians 1:25, Colossians 2:2-3), we should never think our wisdom is somehow greater or more complete, but should be asking for wisdom from Him (James 1:5).

Job has already fallen because of his pride (Proverbs 16:18) and the fall will continue until his words are ended. Furthermore, he has deceived himself with his pride – self-deception being one of the greatest kinds of deception. Between verses 8-12, Job knows that he cannot find God (23:8-9), but that God knows everything that Job does (23:10). Job then claims that he will come through God's test for him as gold because he has loved God's way more than his daily sustenance (23:10-12). I don't think Job is claiming sinless perfection because he knows that he has sinned (14:16), but he is making the claiming that his behavior is so good God could not possibly find fault.

Unfortunately for Job, these statements are quite a sin and they deserve justice from God in whatever severity He chooses. It is true that Job didn't do anything directly that made him deserve his suffering; on the contrary it was his righteousness that caused his condition (1:8, 2:3). We also know that Job will come out of this situation better than when he began (42:7-17). But this refining fire is not without God's intervention. When God tests us, we are not to think we will come forth as gold because of our own past, present, or future works. God is both the Tester and the Refiner, and without Him instructing us we would be part of the dross that is removed from the gold when put through the fire.

Next, Job makes an excuse for why his plan of convincing God won't work and places the blame on God and not himself. Because God does not change (Malachi 3:6) and He does whatever He pleases (Psalm 115:3), Job can't change his situation (23:13-14). This scares Job greatly (23:15-17), and I would be scared too if we had no free choice in anything that happens! While it is true that God is in control of everything (Acts 15:18), it is also true that we can choose to serve God or not (Joshua 24:15). The free will vs. God's sovereignty debate rests on these two seemingly contradictory truths; God is completely in control and we have the freedom to choose.

Rather than going down the rabbit trail of this debate, our application from Job is this: when faced with adversity, we are to cry out to God for help and wisdom rather than depending on ourself or give up hope. Job both depended on himself (23:4-7) and gave up hope of his situation changing (6:11, 30:26), and it is hard to blame him. Yet, these things are written for our benefit, to the intent that we would not walk in the same evil ways (1 Corinthians 10:6).

Job shifts his argument to asking a question that he will answer throughout chapter 24. There are a wide variety of translations of 24:1 within different English translations and the Hebrew is not totally clear to ascertain the correct translation. I believe the KJV and NKJV have it right, with the NKJV reordering the words but making the question slightly clearer than the KJV. To help explain the question, the verse reads in the NKJV:

> Since times are not hidden from the Almighty, why do those who know Him see not his days?
> *24:1*

The KVJ reads:

> Why, seeing times are not hidden from the Almighty, do they that know him not see His days?
> *24:1*

Since Job just finished talking about how God performs all that is appointed for Job, and by extension all men, in verses 13-17 of chapter 23 (remember chapter and verse divisions are not inspired), I believe Job is asking why he doesn't get to see God's days. My attempt at rephrasing the question and making it personal to Job is this: Since God sees all the events of my days, why do I not get to see the events of God's days?

Job spends the rest of chapter 24 pointing out sins the wicked perform and how it impacts others, namely orphans, widows, the poor, the hungry, the needy, and the barren. It can be a bit difficult understanding who a passage is talking about because the pronouns will remain the same but

Job: 23:1-24:25

change between the wicked, downtrodden, and, at the end of the chapter, God. The below chart is helpful to outline the pronoun usage in the chapter:

Verse(s)	Subject	Pronoun(s)
2-4	Wicked	They
5-8	Poor	They
9-10	Wicked	They
11-12	Poor and hungry	They
13-22	Wicked	Those, they, he, me, etc.
23	God	He, His
23	Wicked	They, their
24	Wicked	They

With this understanding, we can continue working through Job's argument.

Job points out specific sins of the wicked, including stealing, murder, and adultery (24:2, 14, 15). He points out the suffering the downtrodden deal with because of these sins (24:4-8, 10-12). Job explains the wicked should be removed from the earth (24:18-22). Job also recognizes that it is God Who gives the wicked their security or prosperity but also watches their ways, indicating He is not going to overlook the justice they deserve (24:23). This justice does eventually come to the wicked (24:24). Job concludes his argument by challenging his three friends to prove him wrong (24:25).

I believe what Job is saying by answering his own question of why he doesn't get to see God's days is, "Why don't I get to know why God allows the wicked to prosper on earth even though they eventually receive justice for their actions?" Job's question is a question of timing of justice rather than questioning whether justice comes at all, which we recognized as the believer's problem of evil from chapter 21.

Unfortunately, or fortunately depending on how you look at it, the answer to Job's question is simple. The emphatic answer from Scripture is no, man does not get to see God's days or why He does what He does. Elihu gives Job this answer in 36:26: "Behold, God is great, and we do not know Him; nor can the number of His years be discovered." God gives a very long explanation of why Job doesn't get to see His days by all the questions He asks Job throughout chapters 38-41. In these chapters, God is explaining His greatness compared to Job, which is the reason Job doesn't get to see His days.

Ecclesiastes, a companion to the book of Job, says:

> Then I saw all the work of God, that a man cannot find out the work that is done under the sun. For though a man labors to discover it, yet he will not find it; moreover, though a wise man attempts to know it, he will not be able to find it.
> *Ecclesiastes 8:17*

Job: 23:1-24:25

Ecclesiastes also says, "who knows what is good for man in life?" (Ecclesiastes 6:12). Also, in Ecclesiastes 2:13, it says, "this burdensome task (all that is done under heaven) God has given to the sons of man by which they may be exercised." This verse is very applicable to Job because he is going through a very difficult workout.

While Elihu and God give Job answers to his question, Job's missing of the mark is explained in Ecclesiastes 3:11: "Also, He has put eternity in their hearts, except that no one can find out the work that God does from beginning to end." Not only does this verse give us a clear answer that we do not get to see God's days but explains that God's work is much bigger than human history on Earth. Job's mistake was that he forgot about eternity. When he considered the justice of the wicked, he did not factor in justice that can happen after death but only looked at what he saw during his life on earth.

Many times throughout our lives we are faced with what looks like injustice, seeing wickedness in the place of justice and iniquity in the place of righteousness (Ecclesiastes 3:16). When we feel like complaining to God like Job did, we should realize that "God shall judge the righteous and the wicked, for there is a time there for every purpose and for every work" (Ecclesiastes 3:17). This "time" extends beyond this present creation and into the final judgement where God will repay everyone, wicked and righteous, according to their work (Revelation

20:11-15, 22:15). May we always seek to understand events from God's perspective, that He is working things out for His own glory (Romans 8:28, Philippians 2:9-11).

Bildad is up next to respond to Job with a very short statement which concludes Job's friends' discourses.

Chapter 19

Bildad Argument 3

25:1-6

Bildad's argument is very short and makes a simple point: Since God is so much greater than man (25:2-3), how can a man be righteous before God (25:4-6)? Job asked the exact same question in 9:2. The implied answer is no, there is no way for man to be righteous before God. And Bildad is absolutely correct.

Except that God loved us so much that He sent His Son to die for us, creating a way for us to be righteous before Him (John 3:16, 2 Corinthians 5:21). When we believe the good news that Jesus died for our sins and rose from the grave, He gives us eternal life because there is nothing we could give Him to be righteous. If you are reading this now and have not believed this message, my prayer for you is that you would place your faith in Jesus as your Savior. And if you have believed this message, I pray that you would constantly be reminded of so great a salvation that we have been given by no effort of our own.

Chapter 20

Job Argument 9

26:1-31:40

Job's last discourse is a long one, spanning six chapters. The chapter divisions are helpful, and each chapter has a different angle in which Job justifies himself. We'll take each point one at a time, much like we broke up Elihu's discourse.

Job's First Theme

Chapter 26 is Job's response to Bildad, with the rest of his discourse not necessarily directly related to his friend's arguments. Job makes a good point that Bildad (and by extension Eliphaz and Zophar) have not helped Job or anyone who is without hope (26:1-4). Job then restates many of the things said about God's majesty throughout the book (26:5-14). Job even makes reference to a serpent, which I believe is a reference to Satan in the Garden, and some facts

85

about Earth's shape, place in outer space, and nature. It doesn't sound like Job is using hyperbole, rather he is speaking authoritatively about God's creation. The facts he explains are corroborated by science, and there should be no way that people living at the time of Job could know these facts. I believe somehow God illuminated these things to people as a way to glorify Himself to His creation.

Ultimately, what I believe Job is saying in response to Bildad is, "Whoop-de-do, I know that God is greater than man. That doesn't answer any of my questions." Job is without hope and telling him that "God is sovereign" or "God is in control" doesn't comfort him or aid in his understanding of why his suffering is taking place. We should take care to not use only these reasonings when comforting or counseling one who is suffering.

Job's Second Theme

Job continues his discourse, now speaking to God as much as his three friends (27:1). Because the argument "God is greater than man" doesn't answer why he is experiencing suffering, Job now turns to justify himself over the wicked.

Job blames God for his troubles, which is true in terms of Who is responsible (2:3), but not in the sense that it is unjust (27:2). Additionally, God does not force anyone to be bitter; Job clearly has the knowledge to respond correctly to his suffering (1:20-

22, 2:10). He has chosen, as we often do, to respond negatively to events in life when we could respond positively. A good example of a correct response is Paul and Silas at Philippi. Instead of being angry at God for the massive beating they endured and being jailed, they were praying and singing praises to God at midnight (Acts 16:16-34)! What a testimony to having a correct attitude in the face of great adversity!

Job then makes one of the most ironic statements in the Bible, that he will never commit any wickedness and hold fast to his righteousness (27:3-6). The irony is that his whole argument is justifying himself rather than God, which is wickedness (32:1-2). If only he took his own advice in 28:28: "the fear of the Lord, that is wisdom, and to depart from evil is understanding." To avoid this boasting in our own lives, Romans 12:16 instructs, "Do not be wise in your own opinion."

Next, Job contrasts himself with the wicked. He begins by saying his enemies should be like the wicked (27:7-10), and then explains what the wicked deserve (27:12-23). He doesn't define exactly who his enemy is, but in context it seems to be anyone that disagrees with him. When Job says in 27:8, "For what is the hope of the hypocrite...?" I believe he is saying, "if I have no hope or prosperity, then I wish for the wicked to have none too." Romans is instructive here as well, explaining what is wrong with thinking this way:

> Repay no one evil for evil... Beloved, do not avenge yourselves, but rather give place to wrath; for it is written, "Vengeance is Mine, I will repay"
> *Romans 12:17, 19*

Job's Third Theme

Job spends chapter 28 talking about wisdom, probably to prove to his friends how smart he is. He spends the first 11 verses setting up his argument by talking about how man explores and manipulates the Earth (28:1-11). Man mines for minerals, cuts paths through mountains, and changes the course of streams. But in all these things, wisdom is not found because it is not something physical (28:12).

Wisdom cannot be compared to any mineral or metal that man finds in the Earth (28:13-19). Throughout Proverbs, Solomon makes the exact same point (Proverbs 3:14-15, 8:10-11, 15:16, 16:16).

Job then asks a simple question: "From where then does wisdom come?" (28:20-23). This is a question that has eluded philosophers for ages, but the answer is very simple and it was solved a long time ago. The source of wisdom is God, and without God, there will never be a source or standard for wisdom. God created wisdom (Proverbs 8:12-31) and if you want to get it (Proverbs 4:5) you must "fear the Lord" (28:23-28). We also must depart from evil to have understanding, which means the opposite of wisdom is not departing from evil (28:28).

Job: 26:1-31:40

Job is exactly correct in everything he says about wisdom and we would be wise to heed his words. Unfortunately, he is not currently fearing the Lord but rather challenging Him. May we always put our faith in God before our self-righteousness.

Job's Fourth Theme

Job goes on a long lament through chapters 29 and 30 about his life before and after the events of Job 1 and 2. He wishes to return to his life "when God watched over [him]" (29:2) and then talks about the great joy, respect, and influence he had in those days (29:3-25). Job was a very good man and we should take him at his word for everything he says he did because God recognized his uprightness (1:8, 2:3). One way to apply everything Job is saying is to test ourselves to see whether we are doing the things that we should (2 Corinthians 13:5). This is not an examination to see whether we are saved or not but a test to see if our lives are aligning with what a righteous life looks like. Job certainly doesn't seem like the book where we would find such a test, but it certainly is a useful way to view chapter 29!

"But now..." (30:1). Usually this is a phase I love to read, because in the New Testament it is often used to contrast our life before salvation with our new birth and sanctification (Romans 3:21). But for Job it is a very debilitating thought of his current life contrasted with the life he just described. He is mocked by those who once respected him (30:1, 9-10) and they have turned aside to evil (30:2-8, 12-15). He believes that their wickedness is partly because of him because he is no longer a positive influence on their life (30:11).

In many ways, Job might be right about this. Proverbs supports the same idea that "where there is no counsel, the people fall" (Proverbs 11:4) and "The righteous should choose his friends carefully, for the way of the wicked leads them astray" (Proverbs 12:26).

However, Job should not feel responsible. God is the one who allowed Satan to test him, and therefore Job was no longer being an influence on these people by no act of his own. Not only could God bring in other positive influences, but the people within Job's influence are also able to choose the right path (Psalm 1:1-2). "The integrity of the upright will guide them" Proverbs 11:3 says. If we are guided by our integrity, which is ultimately our faith in God, then we should always be willing to follow His leading, even if that means leaving something "good" behind.

Because of all his suffering, Job again complains to God about how much affliction he is in (30:16-19). He attributes all of this to God, saying God doesn't hear him, is cruel to him, ruins his success, and will ultimately kill him (30:20-23). Verses 24-31 talk about Job's lack of hope, that even when he is a heap of ruins, God is still against him. Even though Job was a good man, only evil came to him (30:25-31). Job succumbed to the temptation of complaining instead of trusting God even though he had the knowledge and ability to keep trusting God (1 Corinthians 10:13).

Job's Fifth Theme

Job makes one final plea to God by explaining why he should not deserve his affliction. He makes many "if, then" statements about if he had done something wrong, then he would be deserving of his suffering. Job is asking the question "If God sees all my steps (31:4), then why am I suffering?" His examples are improper sexual behavior (31:1, 9-12), lying (31:5-8), treating his servants poorly (31:13-15), treating the poor and widows improperly (31:16-23), worshiping idols or false gods (31:24-28), rejoicing at the destruction of his enemies (31:29-31), not governing his servant correctly (31:31-32), hiding his iniquity (31:33-34), and stealing (31:38-40).

Job says that if any of these things are true God should answer him and write a book of sins not to commit (31:35-37). Thankfully for us, Job's Prosecutor both wrote the Book and answered him! We should never ask for God to "show [us] why He contends with [us]" (10:2) because He just might! And then we would have the same response Job had, which is stop speaking and abhor our behavior (40:5, 42:6).

Thus the (self-righteous) words of Job are ended. But that is not the end of the story.

Chapter 21

Job's Responses to God

40:3-5, 42:42-6

Obviously, Job does not have much to say after God shows him how foolish he was. In 40:3-5, his realizes his evil attitude and knows he cannot respond to anything God says.

In Job's second response, Job has a new level of understanding for God's ability (42:2) and His wisdom (42:3). Job says in 42:5, "I have heard of You by the hearing of the ear, but now my eye sees You." Job has now seen and experienced God and instead of God being more of a concept, He is now more real than He has ever been.

That does not mean that Job did not understand or know who God was before He spoke. A person who has never participated in a race will come to the same feeling that Job is experiencing if they run in one. The runner understood beforehand that the race will be tiring. Even though the knowledge didn't change, experiencing the tiredness during a race brings a new level of understanding.

Paul makes the same point in 1 Corinthians 13:12. For example, we are able to see God's majesty through a mirror dimly in our current life. When we get to Heaven, God will not be any more or less majestic, but we will experience His majesty face to face which will bring a new level of understanding.

Job has now experienced God in a face to face way, not literally but close to it. Now he sees Him better (42:5). This new experiential knowledge causes Job to abhor himself and change his mind (repent) about everything he has said thus far (42:6). May we learn from Job's experience, that the knowledge God gives us through His Word is sufficient to understand Him well enough that we do not justify ourselves rather than God.

Chapter 22

Epilogue

42:7-17

Thankfully, the book does not end with the arguments but concludes with God restoring Job's losses two-fold (42:10). The restoration began after the three friends came to Job with sacrifices and Job prayed for his friends, even though God had already accepted him (42:7-9). All four men had spoken of God incorrectly, and this restoration is similar to what John says of believers keeping their fellowship with God intact: "If we confess our sins, He is faithful and just to forgive us our sins and to cleanse us from all unrighteousness" (1 John 1:9). Job was clearly saved (1:8, 2:3) and I believe that Job's friends were as well, not only because of their knowledge of God but also because God told them to offer sacrifices (42:7-8). God wasn't telling these men how to get saved, just as John was not telling his audience how to get saved, but how to restore fellowship that had been broken by their sin.

The epilogue also settles the argument between God and Satan with which the book began. Satan claimed Job was only upright because God was protecting his household, possessions, and body (1:9-11, 2:4-5). God claimed that Job was upright because of his character, specifically that he feared God and shunned evil (1:8, 2:3). Job must have known this was the source of righteousness as well, because he points out the same two qualities as being wisdom (28:28).

In the end, God was right, and Satan was wrong. Job questioned God and justified himself, but he never cursed Him to His face. Without God intervening, Job may have never been restored and might have continued in his suffering state. But when given the chance, Job responded correctly and changed his mind about his self-righteousness.

As a concluding thought to this magnificent story, we should realize that God is the hero of the book of Job. I believe Job became an even better man after these events, but it was because of God both giving the experience to teach Job and then restoring him. May we always remember to stand still and consider the wonderous works of God and let Him be the hero of our story.

Job Timing Indications

The Bible does not say who wrote Job or when it was written. Because of this, there is no need to be dogmatic about these two facts. We can all be sure that someone wrote it at some point. But the Word of God is meant to be studied, therefore it is worth asking the two questions, "when was Job written?" and "who wrote it?"

When was Job written?

Job gives us a number of clues about the timing of the writing. The strongest evidence for Job's timing is 22:16 in which Eliphaz talks about men "whose foundations were swept away by a flood." In order for Eliphaz to make this statement, he would have to know what a flood was. In 22:15 he mentions "wicked men" and the "old way" which is probably the same "former age" that Bildad referenced in 8:8. What event in history fits these details? The flood of Noah. Elihu mentions rain in 36:27-28, which rain possibly did not happen until the flood. Especially if you combine that with Job knowing that the earth "is turned up as by fire" (28:5) because volcanoes may not have erupted before the flood, I think it's a safe bet to put the events of Job after the flood.

But when after the flood? I think Job's reference to a "fleeing serpent" in 26:13 is talking about Satan in the Garden of Eden, which could indicate that the events were not too far along in history. Shem, who had experienced the "former age" and probably heard stories about the Garden, lived for 502 years after the flood (Genesis 11:10). He surely told stories about flood events, which could have been passed onto Job, even after Shem had died.

Elihu talking about kings and nobles in 34:18 and Job living in the land of Uz (1:1) may indicate that the dispersion at the Tower of Babel already happened. Human government was organized after the flood, and the language confusion at the Tower of Babel created the nations. At this point, kings and nobles may have been created beyond the structure of what Nimrod had organized at Babel (Genesis 10:10). Therefore, Elihu would be familiar with the concept.

I believe this evidence points to the events of Job happening sometime after the Tower of Babel. But when after? Since there are no specific Jewish references in Job other than YHWH being used at various points, the events may have happened before God called Abraham. This also fits Job's probable age at death, somewhere in the low 200's. In order to have ten children that were able to feast together (1:4), Job could have been anywhere between 40 and 70. Job then lived 140 years after his suffering (42:16). That puts his age between 180 and 210.

Another interesting angle is that "the LORD gave Job twice as much as he had before" (42:10). Could this also include his age? If it does, that would mean Job was 70 when the events occurred and then lived twice as long (140 years) after his suffering for a total of 210 years. Men started to live not much beyond 200 years old beginning with Peleg, the 5th from Shem (Genesis 11:16) with Abraham only living 175 years (Genesis 25:7).

I believe this means that the events of Job happened sometime between Peleg's birth and God calling Abraham which would be between 1757 and 2023 CE (~2549 and ~2283 BC). It may be closer to the latter date because of who could have written Job.

Who wrote Job?

Many theories abound about who wrote Job, from Job himself to Solomon to a Jew during the Exile. Whenever studying who wrote a Biblical book, I have always found Romans 3:2 instructive, "Chiefly because to them [Jews] were committed the oracles of God." If we take "oracles" as including Scripture, it would mean every book of the Bible was written by a Jew. The Greek word translated "oracle" means "a brief utterance." If all Scripture is God-breathed (2 Timothy 3:16), then the Jews were committed all the brief utterances of God. Acts 7:38 makes the point that Moses received living oracles to give to the children of Israel. These oracles were written down in the form of the Torah. While I would not break fellowship over this matter, I'm persuaded that all Scripture was written by the Jews and that would mean Job is written by a Jew.

We are not given a lineage of Job, but we are told he lived in the land of Uz. The first Uz mentioned in the Bible was a son of Aram and also the grandson of Shem (Genesis 10:23). There is another Uz that was the son of Dishon the son of Seir, which is the country of Edom or Esau (Genesis 36:28, 1 Chronicles 1:42). Interestingly, another Uz is mentioned as being the son of Shem (1 Chronicles 1:17), but Genesis does not mention Shem having a son named Uz. Jeremiah mentions the land of Uz, which he equates to Edom in Lamentations 4:21. We also know that "Esau is Edom" (Genesis 36:8).

Job probably wasn't Jewish, because he would be mentioned in a Jewish lineage and the timing of Job probably happened around the time of Abraham. But if Job is living in the land of Uz, it is quite possible that he is distantly related to Abraham through either Aram, Shem, or Seir, if we assume Job came from the same family as these.

Examining Job's friends does not give us any clear clues. Esau had a son named Eliphaz through Adah (Genesis 36:4), but the mention of him being a Temanite probable excludes this from being the same Eliphaz. Unfortunately, Zophar, Bildad, and Elihu do not appear as names in Genesis, although there are mentions of Elihus in Samuel and Chronicles, indicating that the name was Jewish (also the construction of the name "Elihu" sounds Jewish, the name meaning "He is my God"). However, Elihu having a Jewish link does not prove anything definitively.

If we put this together, Job could be distantly related to Abraham, Isaac and Jacob and most likely lived about the same time. Job's story circulated through the land of Uz and probably beyond its borders (2:11). One possibility of how Job became a written book was Abraham, Isaac or Jacob traveling to see Job after God has restored him and one of those three putting the story to paper (metaphorically speaking). Abraham could have done this while waiting for Isaac to be born, or Jacob could have traveled to Job after Joseph was taken to Egypt. God could have used Job's story to offer comfort to these men while they had a lack of hope.

I'm aware I'm making many assumptions about the writing of Job, but I believe it's worth studying and thinking about how it came to be written. One thing I can be sure of is it is part of the Word of God and on that we should all agree.

Arguments of Job in Summary Form

Speaker	Verses	Argument
Job	3:1-26	I wish I would have died at birth.
Eliphaz	4:1-5:27	You are suffering because of your wickedness. Become righteous and God will restore you.
Job	5:1-6:30	I am without hope because of God's endless oppression and my friends should comfort me.
Bildad	8:1-22	God does not subvert judgement. Become blameless and God will restore you.
Job	9:1-10:22	God is mighty above man and cannot understand man's plight
Zophar	11:1-20	God is greater than man and can punish without hindrance. Put iniquity away and God will restore you
Job	12:1-14:22	God is all powerful and I will trust Him, yet I will defend my ways.
Eliphaz	15:1-35	Job, you are wicked and your life makes it clear you are wicked.

Arguments of Job in summary form

Job	16:1-17:16	You give me neither hope nor comfort from your words.
Bildad	18:1-21	The dwelling of the wicked is full of destruction and strife.
Job	19:1-29	My life may look like the wicked's, but it is because God has wronged me. But one day I will see God because of my Redeemer.
Zophar	20:1-29	The life of the wicked is full of misery and terror.
Job	21:1-34	Why do the wicked live and become old, yes, become mighty in power? How often is the lamp of the wicked put out? Can anyone teach God knowledge since He judges those on High?
Eliphaz	22:1-30	Job, you have committed awful sins. If you acquaint yourself with God, you can be at peace with Him.
Job	23:1-24:25	If I could find God, I would reason with Him and be delivered. Since God sees all of events of my days, why do I not get to see the events of God's days?

Bildad	25:1-6	Since God is so much greater than man, how can a man be righteous before God?
Job	26:1-14	God is greater than man but that does not answer my questions.
Job	27:1-23	I will hold fast to my integrity and may hypocrites be like the wicked.
Job	28:1-28	The fear of the Lord, that is wisdom.
Job	29:1-30:31	Oh, how I long for the days before my troubles.
Job	31:1-40	If I committed iniquity, then I would be deserving of this punishment.
Elihu	33:1-33	God is greater than man; so He does not have to answer to him.
Elihu	34:1-37	God is the creator; so He always justly repays man according to his work.
Elihu	35:1-16	God is unaffected by man's action; so He will always act justly and at the correct time.
Elihu	36:1-23	God is mighty and shows no favoritism; so He is understanding of everyone's situation.

Arguments of Job in summary form

Elihu	36:24-37:24	God is far beyond man in power; so we should fear and revere Him.
God	38:1-40:2	Can you (Job) do what I have done?
Job	40:3-5	Once I have spoken, but I will not answer.
God	40:6-14	If you have the power, correct what I have done wrong.
God	40:15-41:34	Look at Behemoth and Leviathan to see My majesty.
Job	42:1-6	I now see You. I abhor myself and repent in dust and ashes.

About the Author

Lucas is a bondservant of Jesus Christ.

www.ingramcontent.com/pod-product-compliance
Lightning Source LLC
Chambersburg PA
CBHW020911080526
44589CB00011B/542